WORLDWISE

ANCIENT GREECE

Written by
Nick Pierce

Illustrated by
Beatriz Castro

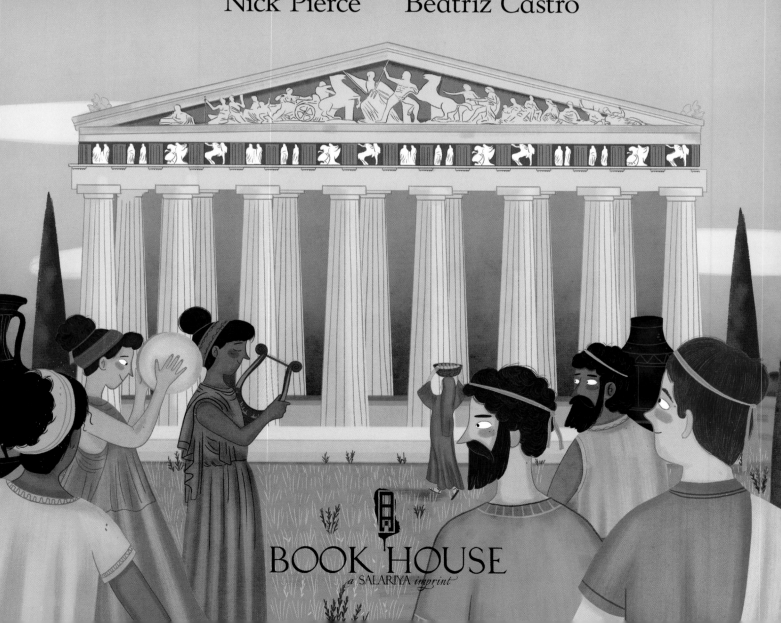

BOOK HOUSE
a SALARIYA *imprint*

This edition first published in MMXIX by
Book House

Distributed by Black Rabbit Books
P.O. Box 3263
Mankato, Minnesota 56002

Cataloging-in-Publication Data is available
from the Library of Congress

Printed in the United States
At Corporate Graphics,
North Mankato, Minnesota

9 8 7 6 5 4 3 2 1

ISBN: 978-1-912233-86-1

Contents

Introduction 4

The Land 6

The Greek World 8

Life in the City 10

The Marketplace 12

Sport in Greece 14

Schools and Education 16

Temples and Religion 18

Timeline 20

Quiz 22

Glossary 23

Index 24

Introduction

The ancient Greeks lived over 2,500 years ago. Greek civilization flourished from around 800–350 BCE. Greek armies were brave and strong. Scholars were clever, craftworkers and artists were skilful, and merchants were rich.

The ancient Greeks' homeland was present-day Greece. But the "Greek world" stretched all around the Mediterranean Sea, from southern Europe to the north of Africa. Many Greek people lived in Cyprus and Turkey, and on islands off the Greek and Turkish coasts. Merchants sailed between these settlements. The Greeks built new towns in southern Italy and on the shores of the Black Sea.

Philip II of Macedon conquered Greek lands in 338 BCE, but Greek civilization did not disappear completely. Today, we still admire many Greek buildings and works of art. We still use some Greek words. And we still rely on many Greek inventions and discoveries.

On each spread you will have to look for different objects in the main picture.

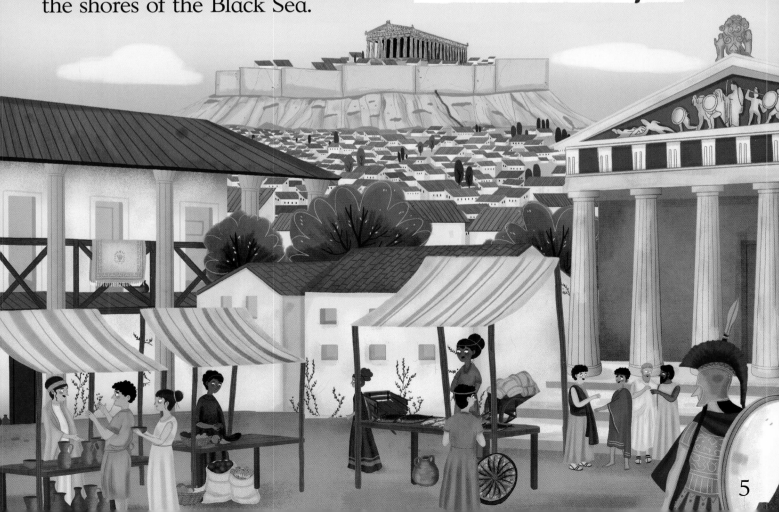

The Land

The land of ancient Greece was very beautiful, with its mountains, forests, cliffs, and streams. But the soil was thin, stony, and unsuitable for most crops except olives, grapes, and grain. Only goats and tough mountain sheep could survive. The climate was also harsh. Summers were very hot, but winters could be bitterly cold.

Can you find...?

▲**Olives**
At harvest time, the whole family worked hard to collect ripe olives. They pressed them to make into oil.

▲**Animals**
Sheep, goats, pigs, and cattle were raised for their meat.

▲**Farmhouses**
Greek farmhouses were made of rough stone, with clay tile roofs. Windows had strong wooden shutters to keep out thieves.

The Greek World

Can you find...?

▼Swords
How many swords can you count in this picture?

Ephebes
At the age of 18, Greek men became "ephebes." This meant they were ready to become citizens, but first they had to prove themselves worthy. Ephebes had to live by strict rules for two years which included a period of military service.

▼Weapons
Greek soldiers fought with sharp iron swords, long, bronze-tipped spears, and wooden shields. Weapons, helmets, and armor were passed on proudly from father to son.

◀Shields
Can you find this shield in the picture?

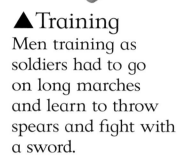

▲Training
Men training as soldiers had to go on long marches and learn to throw spears and fight with a sword.

▼Helmets
How many helmets can you count in this picture?

Greek city-states were often at war. They fought against one another, but they also united to fight together against enemies from abroad. All ephebes, or men over 18, were expected to join the army. In Athens, recruits had to spend two years training. Greek soldiers fought mostly on foot. In battle, they advanced in close ranks called a "phalanx." This formation presented a wall of shields to the enemy. Soldiers from opposing phalanxes threw spears at one another, hoping to make the enemy soldiers run off.

Professionals
Some city-states had professional soldiers, recruited from nearby lands. They fought with slingshots (strips of fabric for hurling stones) or with bows and arrows.

Can you find...?

Life in the City

▲Foreigners
Many non-Greek peoples also lived in Greek cities. No foreigner, woman, or child had citizens' rights.

In early Greek times, most people lived and worked in the countryside. But from around 700 BCE, they started to move to the cities. They found they could make a better living there, as shopkeepers, butchers, bakers, entertainers, and craftworkers of all kinds. Cities were busy, noisy, crowded, and often very smelly. Overcrowding led to quarrels, riots, food shortages, and disease.

▲Temple
The Greek city of Athens had fine temples, theaters, sports halls, schools, government offices, shops, and taverns.

◀Citizen Soldiers
Citizen soldiers kept guard outside the city gates and on the city walls.

◀Citizens
Can you find these city-dwellers in the picture?

▲The poor
The houses of the poor in Greek cities were packed tightly together. There, citizens lived in simple single-storey homes.

▲The rich
Wealthier citizens lived in well-planned homes, with rooms for preparing and cooking food, and for entertaining their many guests.

▶The Parthenon
The Parthenon (built 447–438 BCE) was a temple dedicated to the goddess Athena.

The Marketplace

Can you find...?

▲Take-out
In big towns, the market stalls sold take-out foods.

▲Slaves
Men or slaves usually did all the shopping. Servants and slaves carried water from street fountains. "Respectable" women usually stayed at home.

◀Food
Farmers brought eggs and chickens to sell. There was no room in the city to grow food.

◀Food
Can you find this basket of food in the picture?

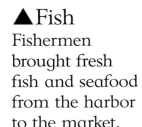

▲Fish
Fishermen brought fresh fish and seafood from the harbor to the market.

The marketplace was the social center of each Greek city. Citizens went there every day to buy food. They also went to the market to meet their friends to discuss local politics and the latest news. City-states grew rich by taxing trade. So they encouraged trade by building new markets, with rooms nearby where bankers and money-changers could work.

▲Dog
Can you spot the dog?

▶Haggling
Buyers and sellers haggled over prices. Everyone wanted a bargain.

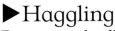

Sport in Greece

Sport was important to the Greeks. It was fun and it was good training for war, too. Soldiers built up their strength by running in armor, throwing spears, wrestling, and boxing. These sports were all useful when it came to fighting real enemies. The Olympic Games took place over five days, every four years. Victorious sportsmen won fame and fortune. They were crowned with an olive wreath, and given prizes of olive oil, fine fabrics, and pottery. Poems were also written in their praise.

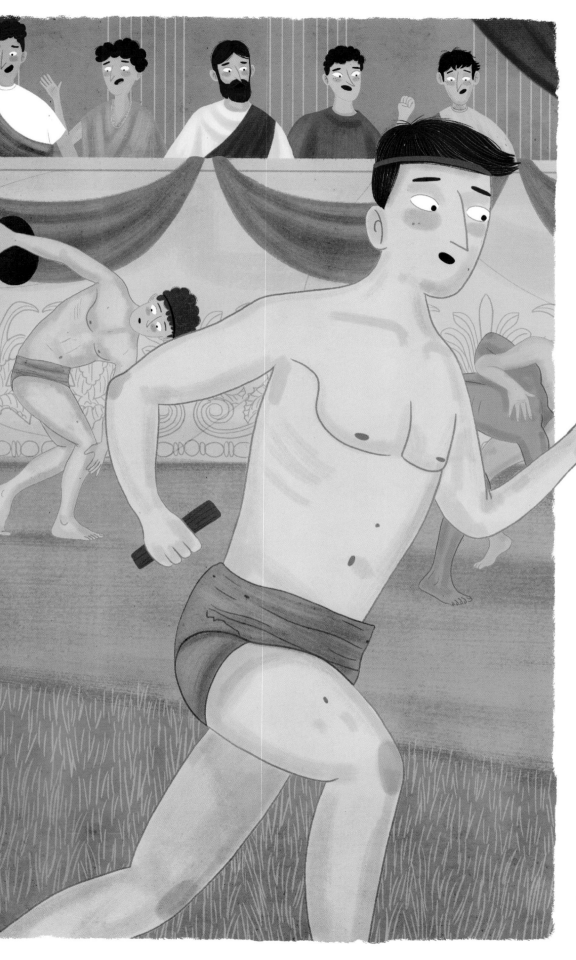

Can you find...?

▲Discus

Discus was one of the events in the Greek Olympics. Contestants had to throw the disc as far as possible.

▲Stadium

The stadium in Olympia where races were held was almost 656 feet (200 meters) long and 98 ft (30 m) wide.

Holy site

Olympia was an ancient holy site. Games were first held there in 776 BCE, in honor of the god Zeus.

Schools and Education

Can you find...?

▲Pottery
Black-figure pottery was the first painting technique used by Athenian potters.

▲Teacher
Home teachers were very strict. The main focus of a pupil's education revolved around Greek history, which meant learning large amounts of philosophy and poetry by heart.

◀Pupil
For many centuries, the Greek language was not written down.

16

◀Greek women
Greek women were valued for what they did for others, like being faithful to their husbands and creating a comfortable home.

▲Dancing
Girls were trained to dance. Dancing was good exercise and formed an important part of many festivals.

▼Lyre
Popular instruments included lyres, flutes, panpipes, tambourines, and the kithara—an early form of the guitar.

Greek boys were educated differently from girls. Rich boys went to school to learn reading, writing, dancing, music, and maths. Older boys might also study science, philosophy, or law. Exercise was an important part of their education, too. Boys from ordinary families were trained by their fathers in farming, trading, or craft skills. All Greek girls were educated at home. Rich girls learned how to manage a household and how to give orders to slaves. Ordinary girls learned cooking, cleaning, weaving, and childcare.

Temples and Religion

Religious festivals played an important part in many Greek cities. They were held to honor all the different gods or goddesses. Sometimes, festivals were held in memory of ancient local heroes, as well. Nobody worked on festival days. Instead, they said prayers at the temple, or danced, or played music in processions through the streets. People brought offerings, such as animals adorned with garlands of flowers, to give to the gods and goddesses.

▲Gods
Ancient Greeks
believed in many
different gods and
goddesses. Some
brought love and
wealth, and others
caused war and
death. People
brought offerings to
them in the hope
that the gods might
help them.

▼Temples
Elegant temples
were designed with
rows of columns to
support a massive
roof. They were
decorated with
many fine carvings.

19

Timeline

2900 BCE
Early Greek cultures begin to emerge.

750 BCE
The epic poems *The Iliad* and *The Odyssey* are first written down around this time.

776 BCE
The first Olympic Games are held in ancient Greece.

508 BCE
"Democracy" becomes established in the Greek city-state of Athens. Male citizens are given the right to vote to decide how Athens is run.

472 BCE

Theater becomes popular in Athens. Many great plays written around this period are still performed today.

338 BCE

Philip II of Macedon conquers Greece, and his son, Alexander the Great, controls it after his death.

432 BCE

Construction of the Parthenon in Athens is finished.

146 BCE

Greece is conquered by the Romans and becomes part of the Roman Empire.

Quiz

1. What crop is pressed to make oil?

2. What name was given to Greek men when they reached the age of 18?

3. Which famous Greek temple is dedicated to the goddess Athena?

4. Who did most of the shopping in Greece?

5. How many days did the Olympic Games last for, every four years?

6. What is the name of the battle formation of close ranks of foot soldiers?

7. What were animals decorated with for religious festivals?

8. What was the name of the holy site where the Olympic Games were first held?

9. Who did not have citizens' rights in ancient Greece?

10. Who conquered Greece in 338 BCE?

Answers:
1. Olives
2. Ephebes
3. Parthenon
4. Men and slaves
5. Five days
6. Phalanx
7. Flower garlands
8. Olympia
9. Foreigners, women, and children
10. Philip of Macedon

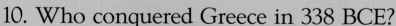

Glossary

Citizen Adult male living in a city-state who had the right to take part in political decision-making.

City-state A self-governing city.

Civilization A society with its own laws, customs, beliefs, and artistic traditions.

Democracy A government where the people rule.

Mediterranean Sea A sea joined to the Atlantic Ocean, almost entirely surrounded by land. It is bordered by southern Europe and North Africa.

Offerings Goods given to please gods and goddesses when asking for help or giving thanks for their blessing.

Phalanx Row of foot-soldiers standing with their shields.

Philosophy The study of ideas.

Scholar Someone who is very educated and knowledgeable about a specific subject.

Slaves Men, women, and children who are not free, but are owned by other people.

Index

A
Athens 9, 10, 20, 21

B
bankers 13

D
democracy 20, 23
discus 15

E
ephebes 8, 9

M
market 12, 13
Mediterranean Sea 5, 23

O
olives 6, 7, 14
Olympic Games 14, 15 20

P
Parthenon 5, 23
phalanx 9, 23
Philip II of Macedon 5, 21
philosophy 16, 17, 23
pottery 14, 16

S
slaves 12, 17, 23

T
teachers 16
temples 10, 11, 18, 19